Grand Slam Man

Published by Accent Press Ltd – 2013

ISBN 9781908917539

The Quick Reads project in Wales is an initiative coordinated by the Welsh Books Council and supported by the Welsh Government.

Printed and bound by CPI Group (UK) Ltd, Croydon, CR0 4YY

Cover design by Madamadari

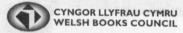

CYNGOR LLYFRAU CYMRU
WELSH BOOKS COUNCIL

Noddir gan
Lywodraeth Cymru
Sponsored by
Welsh Government

Grand Slam Man

Dan Lydiate

ACCENT PRESS LTD

Chapter One

A LUCKY MAN

When I look back on my Grand Slam year, I consider myself a very lucky man. To have won the Slam with Wales and be named Six Nations Player of the Tournament is the kind of stuff dreams are made of.

But then, I have more reason than most to feel lucky.

Back in November 2007, I suffered an injury that could have ended my rugby career.

I was only nineteen at the time and had just started playing for the Newport Gwent Dragons. So when I was selected to play against Perpignan in a big Heineken Cup match out in France I was very excited.

But within minutes of the kick-off, my world was turned upside down. I can still remember exactly how it happened. I'd come across the field to tackle one of their players and after tackling him ended up sitting on the ground. Then everyone piled over me and my head snapped forward. I heard a big crunch in my neck and thought, 'That's not good.' I wasn't knocked unconscious, so I tried to get up. But I couldn't, and I was losing the feeling in my legs and arms. So I tried to keep them moving because I thought that if I stopped I wouldn't be able to get them going again. I was thinking: 'Will I be able to walk again? Will I be able to lead a normal life?' It was pretty scary, and rugby went to the back of my mind.

Dee Clark, the Dragons' team doctor, came running on to the pitch and looked after me, and I realise now that if it had to happen, this was the best place it could have happened. All the medical facilities were on hand and from the start the treatment I had was second to none. It turned out I had suffered a crushed disc, broken vertebrae and ripped a load of ligaments. I had broken my neck. I now appreciate just how lucky I was to receive such excellent care from the Dragons' medical staff and everyone else who looked after me.

After a few days' treatment in France, I was flown back to Wales in an air ambulance. I was wearing a special cast that locked my jaw together to stop me moving my neck. Once back in Wales, I was transferred to Morriston Hospital in Swansea to undergo surgery. It was made clear to me that if I didn't have an operation I would definitely never be able to play rugby again and I could be paralysed by the smallest of falls. During a five-hour operation, they removed the crushed disc in my neck and replaced it with a bone graft from my hip, inserting a plate in my neck. They basically screwed me back together.

Happily, the surgery was a success. The surgeon, John Martin, did a great job. Once I'd had the operation, they said there was no reason why I couldn't play again. So I began to think about the next step on the recovery trail and I started building from there.

I'd only played a handful of games for the Dragons and I'd really enjoyed them. I'd had a taste of the game and wanted more. That's what spurred me to get back into it. I went for regular check-ups at the hospital and X-rays every six weeks. It was a case of seeing how things went. But by the new year, I was exercising my legs and on the road to recovery.

The toughest thing was seeing the Dragons playing on television. That really got to me. Also in January, I went down to Rodney Parade to watch the return match against Perpignan, and that was quite emotional.

So it was tough at times, but I had a lot of support from my family, the doctors and the people at the Dragons. My family were obviously a bit worried about me playing again, but supported whatever I decided. In fact my mum still worries now when anyone goes down and is nervous when I play, as is my girlfriend Nia, but she still comes to watch the games with my dad.

It was a long road back for me, and a lot of work along the way, but by September 2008 I was back on the field. I was nervous at the start, but as soon as I got the first tackle out of the way I was OK.

People have said to me that I was unlucky to get injured when I'd just started my career. But I really count my blessings. The injury could have been so much worse. Not just a case of not playing rugby again, I might not have been able to walk again. So, I do definitely feel lucky.

What happened to me is one of those things that happens a fair bit in rugby. I was at the Millennium Stadium a couple of years ago when the Scotland winger Tom Evans suffered a broken neck against Wales, an injury which ended his career. It happened when he collided with Lee Byrne's hip. You wouldn't have thought that could have done the damage that it did.

Then there was the case of Matt Hampson, the prop from Leicester, who was paralysed after a scrum collapsed in training. He must have hit a scrummaging machine hundreds of times before that and gone into countless scrums, but that one day something happened.

On the other hand, sometimes you see a tackle and hear the impact and you think that player's in trouble, but he just jumps right back up and carries on with the game.

The game we play is a dangerous sport. Players are so strong and so powerful now and the collisions are so big. But the fact is that you can get hurt in any walk of life. When I went to Morriston to have my surgery, there was a bloke in there recovering from the same operation. He actually had fractures at two levels in his neck. I asked him how he did it and he said he'd been shopping! He was filling his car up with bags and as he pulled the boot down it hit him on his head! These things just happen in life. People break bones. The chances are I will break a few more bones along the way, but that's life. You can get knocked down crossing the road.

I don't often think about my accident these days. You soon forget bad times. The only time I've thought about it in the last year or so was when I went back out to Perpignan to play for the Dragons last season. It was the first time I had been back there since I got injured.

Before the game, we went into the stadium for a walk through and I walked over to where it had happened on the pitch. During that whole trip I was remembering things from four years earlier, conversations and images which I hadn't remembered since. It triggered so many memories.

When I walked into the changing room before the game, I looked at where I had sat the previous time. They put the jerseys up and I was seated opposite where I had changed before. I was glad I wasn't in the same place. I was captain of the Dragons that day and before the game I was trying to give my skipper's speech. But I had demons in my head. I shouldn't have been captain really.

We lost the game, but I was happy just to get through it uninjured and walk back into the changing rooms. And I thought to myself, 'That's it, that's that put to bed.'

A lot has happened to me since that day in Perpignan in 2007. And certainly when you achieve something after adversity, it does make it all the sweeter.

When you start playing rugby, your aim is to play for Wales. But when an injury like that happens, you are happy just to walk again. Then, once you re-start training, you get the bug again, and again start wondering, 'What if?'

When I first got capped, I came on for ten minutes against Argentina, and I had to go back out and do fitness training after the match because I'd been on for such a short time. It was hard work, but I was running with a smile on my face because of the feeling that I'd done it. I'd achieved one of my goals.

However, as soon as you get your first cap, you want more. You get the taste, and you to want to win things. For me, that desire to win climaxed last year when we beat France at the Millennium Stadium to complete the Six Nations Grand Slam. When the final whistle went, I felt very emotional. Standing there, having won the Grand Slam, was a really big moment. After everything I had been through, it just meant so much, and I realised again what a lucky man I am.

Chapter Two

THE SLAM BEGINS – WITHOUT ME

Going into the 2012 Six Nations, there was a lot of expectation on Wales. We'd had a lot of praise for what we'd achieved in the 2011 Rugby World Cup out in New Zealand, where we'd finished fourth. The World Cup was a brilliant experience, but I felt we could have done much more. And it was really hard to go out the way we did, losing the semi-final to France by just one point.

So as a group of players, we felt quite disappointed coming home. We'd had a really good chance and chances don't come around that often. It was an opportunity missed. However, there was a lot of praise for us in the press, with people saying that this was the team for the future. But as players you don't just want to be talked about. You want to win things! The only place to do your talking is on the field and we'd lost that semi-final.

The bunch of boys who are with Wales at the moment are all pushing towards the same goal. When we are in training, we really spur each other on and it's a great environment to be in. So there was pressure on us going into the Six Nations, from inside the camp as much as from outside.

But we were full of confidence. The build-up to the World Cup, with all the months of training and fitness work, had put us in such a good place. Whoever we were up against, we believed we could beat them. So everyone was looking forward to the opening game of the championship against Ireland and determined to make a good start.

Unfortunately, I wasn't going to be part of that Dublin match. It's funny really what happened, although it didn't feel funny at the time. In the first game I had for the Dragons after coming back from the World Cup, I got injured against Italian team Prato. Their blindside flanker tackled me and I hurt my ankle as I went down. That put me out for a couple of weeks. Then, towards the end of January, Prato came over for the return and guess what?

The same guy tackled me again and exactly the same thing happened! It was Sod's Law! If I ever come across him again, I'll try and run away from him!

I was really fed up leaving the field that day because I didn't know how bad it was or how long I would be out for, and I knew the Six Nations was coming up. However, Wales still took me to their pre-tournament training camp in Poland and I was able to do a fair amount of work off my feet. I was in the pool every day and it's just good to be in that environment, even if you are injured. You want to push on.

The Welsh medical staff are world class. They proved that with the work they did with me in the World Cup to get me back to fitness after another ankle injury. Me and my ankle! If there is any chance of getting you back fit to play, they will get you there. It's hard for a player, trying to come back after injury. Any chance you get to be involved, you always say you'll play. And in every game, all the boys are carrying injuries. You've always got some little niggle or pain. That's just the physical nature of the sport. I really wanted to play against Ireland, but because I wasn't quite right, I could have missed a tackle where they scored a try. I could have made a fool of myself and been dropped right out of the team and had to wait another year to get my place back. I wasn't quite ready so I had to miss out, with Ryan

Jones coming in at No 6. It's just one of those things.

I didn't travel to Dublin for the game. I had had an injection in my ankle to kill the pain, so I basically had my feet up for three days, just stewing in my house in Newport, and ended up watching the match on television.

I don't like watching games, especially when it's your team that's playing. It kills you, watching it. I'm not a good spectator and I was on tenterhooks the whole game. You almost break into a sweat because you know what the players are going through, and go through it with them, blow for blow.

In fact it turned out to be a really exciting match, although it just about wrecked me. A real cliff-hanger, with the lead swinging to and fro. In the end, it all hinged on a penalty from the Wales full-back Leigh Halfpenny, with just a couple of minutes left. If he kicked it, we would win the game. If he missed, we would lose. No pressure then! But if there's anybody you'd want in that situation it's Leigh. Sometimes I think there's something not quite right with that guy! He's the most professional person you could meet. He's always practising and he always stays behind after training to do extra work on his kicking. During the World Cup semi-final against France, he had been just short with a long-range penalty which would have won the game, and it really cut him up that he missed that. It was a hard kick and he came close, so nobody blamed him at all. But he blamed himself. That's the kind of guy he is. He's a perfectionist.

Ever since that kick, he'd told himself that if he was ever in that position again, he was going to nail it. So he worked at it and worked at it in training. After a session, I would ask him, 'How did it go today?' and he would say, 'Oh, I got every one.' But he wouldn't make any fuss about it. That's just the standard he sets for himself.

With Leigh in the team, if you win a penalty, you basically know that's three points, which is brilliant.

But he'd only just taken over the goal-kicking duties when we were awarded that penalty against Ireland. I don't know what his nerves were like stepping up for that kick, but I know mine were in shreds. I watched that kick through my fingers.

But he held his nerve and it was fantastic to see the ball going over.

It was great for Leigh, especially after the one he just failed with against France. I was so pleased for him. The pressure was on again, but he'd nailed it. It meant we had won the game 23–21 and it was a fantastic start to the Six Nations. The team had kept giving everything right to the end and showed just how much they wanted it. They'd come through and were brilliant.

When the whistle went, I was so disappointed that I wasn't there. I saw all the boys run on the pitch to celebrate and I just wanted to be there and in the changing rooms afterwards.

When you are on the field, it's the hardest place in the world to be. You are giving your all, someone is trying to run over you, you are trying to hurt them. And, in international rugby, you are digging in from the first minute, it is so hard. But at the end, if you have given everything and you know your team-mates realise that, you get huge pleasure from doing it. After the final whistle goes, you walk back into the changing rooms and if you've had a good game, you can put your feet up and start playing the game back in your head.

I did have my feet up after that Ireland game, but not for the reason I would have wanted. Missing that first match of the championship was very hard. So I faced a double battle. A battle to get back to fitness and a battle to get back into the team.

Chapter Three

BACK ON BOARD

The day after the Ireland game, I went up to Wales' base at the Vale Resort just outside Cardiff to do a running test with the physios. I came through OK and our medical manager Prav Mathema said he was happy for me to get back into training with the rest of the squad, which was great news. It made me feel that all the effort I had put in after picking up the injury was worthwhile. Even so, I iced my ankle every two hours for the next three days to bring the swelling down. This meant setting my alarm to go off every couple of hours during the night! (I'd done the same when I was injured during the group stage of the World Cup. I'd been close to being sent home then, but I had been determined to give myself every chance to stay on and remain involved. It paid off then and it was the same story now.)

I was really excited to be back in training because I knew there would be a good buzz with the boys after the result in Dublin. But I was also very nervous for my place, because Ryan Jones had been superb on the blindside flank in my absence. The amount of work he'd got through was unbelievable. He carried, tackled and hit so many rucks. He is a workaholic and did everything that was asked of him. He would have wanted to make his chance count, and he did. I thought he should have got the Man of the Match award.

His form had also been awesome for both club and country in the last season. Whatever position they put him in, he always played well and of course he's such a good guy to have in the squad. He's been Welsh captain, he's a leader, and when he speaks all the boys listen.

So I was very nervous about being selected for the next game against Scotland. You are never sure of your place in this Wales set-up because there's so much competition. You've got to be on your toes the whole time. But that's a good thing. The strength and depth of the squad is great for the coaches. Whoever takes that jersey, they know they are going to perform because they are dying to wear it. And the guys know that if they don't perform there's someone else there that will!

There's just such strength in depth now in

all the positions in the Welsh team. When someone gets injured, another guy comes in, takes his place and is more than likely to have a storming game. Ryan did just that.

Luckily, our head coach Warren Gatland gave me the nod when he read out the team to face Scotland in the second championship match. Ryan had been moved into the second row to replace Bradley Davies, who had been suspended, and I was back in at blindside flanker. I was relieved to say the least. I had my chance now, so I needed not just to have a good game, but a really good game. I was still carrying my ankle a bit. I had it all strapped up, and thankfully it lasted all right and I got a full game under my belt.

So it was really a case of getting back into the groove. There is a big difference between playing regional rugby and Test match rugby, and it's a matter of getting up to speed. Once you get your first tackle out of the way, it's better.

But it is tough when you have been out for a few weeks. I remember thinking at half-time, 'God, I am feeling this already', but I managed to get through the rest of the game OK. The game was in the balance at half-time, but we pulled away after the break, with Leigh Halfpenny scoring two tries after the Scots had a couple of players sin-binned. Yellow cards are always crucial in the game. You've got to be squeaky-clean these days and discipline is so important. We took advantage of those Scottish sin-bins and really took control of the match.

It's not the only time in the last year when we've come on strong in the second half. But it's not really a case of us changing our game or stepping up. We simply play the same game for eighty minutes. Maybe other teams drop off in the last ten minutes, which we used to in the past. But because we are so much fitter now, we just carry on playing the same game. So it looks as though we are stepping up in the last ten but we are not, it's the opposition falling away. Having that fitness in the tank gives you real self-belief.

We ended up winning 27–13, with Leigh having another game to remember, finishing with 22 points in front of a packed Millennium Stadium. And I was named Man of the Match!

We were delighted with the win and with two victories under our belt, we were building real confidence for our next game, against England. You train hard with Wales, but it makes a difference when you are winning because there are smiles on your faces. Even if you are getting exhausted in training, it makes it worthwhile.

Personally, I'd been happy enough with my performance, but you still end up hoping that you've done enough to get picked for the next game.

I wasn't the only Wales player to have come back in against Scotland after injury. Our prop Gethin Jenkins had also missed the opening game out in Ireland, with Rhys Gill doing a good job on the loose head to provide more proof of our strength in depth. Gethin is the moaner in the camp, but I think that's what makes him who he is. If you make a mistake on the field, he's the first to run up to you and call you everything under the sun, just because he wants the best and he wants us to win. The first time I met him I thought, 'Oh this guy really hates me.' But he's like that with everyone! And once you earn his respect, he's fine with you and now we get on really well.

Gethin has been a fixture in the Wales front row for a long time now, as has his fellow prop Adam Jones. The Bomb, as we know Adam, just gets on with his business and he is the best in the world at it, in my view. He's second to none when it comes to scrummaging. All I want from my tight-head is for him to lock out the scrum and hit rucks. When it comes to looking at the stats on a Monday morning, Adam is always up there with the rucks he hits and he's a rock in the scrum. In terms of a person doing their job to a T, he's probably the best on the field. That's all you can ask. He's such a lovely guy as well.

He and Gethin are like chalk and cheese in terms of personalities, but it just seems to work. Going into last season's Six Nations, they'd already got two Grand Slams under their belts and now another one was on its way.

Chapter Four

TRIPLE CROWN TIME

The build-up to the third game of the Six Nations championship against England was a weird time. Wales had only won once at Twickenham in twenty-four years, and yet as we prepared to head up to London we were being tipped as hot favourites. Some people were even suggesting it was a done deal and that we were certain to secure the victory that would win us the Triple Crown. We knew differently.

Going into the match, we were confident, but by no means did we think we would thump them, even if that's always what you want to do. This was England's first home game in the championship and we knew they would come out all guns blazing. It was going to be a massive test for us.

The English are big men and so physical. I think in the future they are going to be a real force. Like us, they are a young squad, and in the next couple of years they will really come into form.

We knew going up there it was going to be a battle, and it was. It was the toughest game of the championship for me. I was aching for days afterwards. All the boys were battered and bruised.

We always knew it would be close and it proved to be one hell of a Test match. I'd never played up in Twickenham before in the Six Nations, and it was an awesome experience to go in on the bus. There was a great atmosphere, with loads of Welsh fans around, and you knew this was going to be a special occasion.

The game was hard and physical from the outset. Our skipper Sam Warburton hurt his knee early on, but strapped it up and just dug in. He was desperate to stay on, especially after coming off at half-time in Ireland. You don't want to give anyone a chance to take your shirt and, in Sam's case, his understudy on the openside flank, Justin Tipuric, had been playing so well. 'Tips' had had an awesome game when he came on against Ireland.

There's so much competition for places in the squad that the boys just dig in and play through the pain. That's why the team is so good to belong to. The guy next to you is going through the same pain as you are, and he's willing to put his body on the line, so you don't mind doing it either.

I always room with Sam when I am away with Wales. Numbers six and seven usually room together, so there's always a lot of banter between us. He's a quality player. He's been a bit unlucky with injuries this last year or so, but I think that's a knock-on effect from how he plays. He punches well above his weight for his size and he always puts his body on the line. Sooner or later it does catch up with you and you miss games. But when he's fit I think he's the best seven in the world. He's also a great skipper, because he leads by example. He may not say much but I don't think he has to. It's more a case of 'Follow me, boys.' That's all I want from my captain.

Sam had a fantastic game that day at Twickenham, even though he was virtually playing on one leg. He led from the front and was quite rightly named Man of the Match. After about half an hour, he put in a crucial tackle on Manu Tuilagi when the powerful England centre looked certain to score a try. There was a stoppage of play after that and I remember watching a re-run on the big screen and thinking that was one hell of a tackle. He had no right to make it really, but he just dived head first at Tuilagi's legs and hauled him down. It was a fantastic effort and part of a great all-round performance from Sam on the day.

The other member of the back row through the Grand Slam campaign was my Dragons team-mate Toby Faletau.

Toby is a law unto himself. It takes a while to get chatting to him because he's not only the politest guy you'd ever want to meet, he's also really shy. He does his talking by the way he plays. He is a world-class No 8 and he's only going to develop more. I don't know what he's made of, but the way he copes with the physical demands of the game is incredible. I'll say to him the day after a game, 'How's your body feeling?' and he'll say, 'Oh, I'm all right,' while I'm thinking, 'I'm in bits here!'

Toby prefers to stay out of the limelight. When he played for the Dragons last season, he was getting Man of the Match week after week. But I think he'd rather not have had it, because it meant he had to do a TV interview after each game!

He's just a really humble guy. The more time you spend with him, the more you realise he's a good boy. It's great to have people like him in the squad.

I really like playing with Sam and Toby. We seem to complement each other. The back row is such a big part of the game. If you can get on top of your opponents in that area it goes a fair way to winning the match. So you need balance. You need a six who does a lot of tackling and hits quite a few rucks, a seven who scavenges for the ball, and a No 8 who is the main ball carrier. That's a good back row and I like to think we've got that with myself, Sam and Toby.

Those two guys were fantastic at Twickenham, where our victory was based on digging deep and taking our chances when they came. We looked in a bit of trouble when our fly-half Rhys Priestland was sin-binned just after half-time. In the past, when we have gone down to fourteen men we have been punished, so this time we really tried to tighten things up. We looked to keep hold of the ball and it was the pick-and-go area that was key. That period was crucial and it meant we were still in the game going into the closing stages.

Then it was 'super sub' Scott Williams who took the chance that mattered, producing the individual moment of the match, four minutes from time. Scott ripped the ball off Courtney Lawes, chipped ahead and won the race to touch the ball down. When he scored the try, I was still on the 22 just waving him on! It was a great effort.

That key contribution from Scott again shows the strength in depth we have. He had come off the bench to replace the injured Jamie Roberts in the centre and he ended up winning the game for us. In our team you just know whoever comes on in a game is going to do a good job, and that keeps you on your toes for your place!

Scott's try put us in front 19–12, but there was still work to do and a dramatic finish to come.

We had managed to shut England out in terms of tries, but it was touch and go at the end.

In the last minute of the game, the England winger David Strettle went over in the corner.

I was running across the field and I didn't think it was a try. But the decision went up to the video referee and it was an agonising wait. We were desperate to know, but because the video screens are so high up you can't really see from the pitch. I couldn't make it out either way and I was just praying for the ref to signal 'no try' and blow his whistle for the end of the game.

When he eventually did, I was so happy. I'd never won any silverware and to win the Triple Crown at Twickenham was just brilliant. It was an awesome feeling for all of us. And walking around the field afterwards with the trophy was a really good feeling. That day will stay as a massive highlight of my career. It's why you play the game: to be at the highest level and win the top prizes.

After the match, we had to go for ice treatment in our mobile cryotherapy unit, which was in the parking lot. We got out there OK, but on the way back the fans spotted us, so everybody wanted a picture. I remember walking back in as Sam was walking out. I said, 'I wouldn't bother if I was you. You'll never get out of there.' I think he just had an ice pack!

That whole day was a great experience. We had won the Triple Crown. But there was still a bigger prize to go for.

Chapter Five

ITALIAN JOB DONE

After the victory over England, we had two games left, against Italy and France, and both of them were at home. I think nearly everybody in Wales was talking Grand Slam.

But I don't think the players were, because we are all pretty grounded. We take each game as it comes. We are not stupid and we treat each match on its own merits. We knew that we might have lost out in Ireland and indeed against England.

So we were keeping our feet on the ground and not getting carried away. However, there was still a buzz in the camp and a good feeling going into the next game against Italy.

But we knew we were in for a battle. In Rome, Italy had given England a really tough match. You always have to contain their massive pack and that is never easy. It was a game which, if we'd just won by just a point, we would have been happy.

However, I always like playing against Italy

because of their back row. I think Sergio Parisse, their No 8, is class. You always want to play against people like that. He's a real power player who is very dangerous. That is why you play the game, to play against the best players in the world.

So we knew it would be another massive physical battle against Italy, particularly up front, and it certainly was that, especially in the first half. They had a young seven by the name of Simone Favaro playing and he was really good at the tackle area. He won quite a few turnovers and he was very strong too. I remember when, from a shortened line-up, he took it up and I hit him as hard as I could. As I was getting up off the floor, I was thinking 'My shoulder is hanging off here!'

You always know you are going to have a lot of bruises after games, but that's good. Every bump and bruise is worth it when you win. In the back row, we like to pride ourselves on being physical and destructive. When you come up against teams with a similar nature you lift your game to your best. It's a macho thing, you want to give as good as you get.

This was another game that was pretty tight at half-time. There hadn't been a try and we were only 9–3 up. But then, after the break, Jamie Roberts ran in from a long way out. I didn't think he was going to get there because he started to slow up, but he made it. Jamie is a big character and a big player for us. He was struggling with his knee during the Six Nations and had to have an operation at the end of the season. But he managed to get through the championship and he did a great job for us.

He and Jonathan Davies have got a great partnership going in the centre. They have got the skills to give you that all-important go-forward. They are big men, bigger than a lot of the forwards. Real battering rams.

Jonathan Davies had a hell of a season last year. He's a quality player. A lot of the time his work goes unseen. He's a world-class defender and such a strong guy. When he tackles, he really hits people. But he's also got the speed and the hands. He scored some quality tries last season, including two in the championship opener against Ireland, and it was good to see him get the recognition he deserves.

It's an awesome experience to be involved with our squad. We work hard, but we always have a good laugh. Everyone enjoys good company and to have a good bunch of mates around you all the time is important. If we didn't like each other I think that would show on the pitch. It would become hard work. It's odd – because the squad is so young it doesn't feel like a proper international team. It feels more as if we're an age-group side, where everyone's working for each other. Putting on the jersey means so much to all of us and because we spend so much time with each other – not just players but the coaches and everyone else – we all become good mates, on and off the field. I think that is why we gel so well as a team. It's almost a family environment.

Things just seemed to click for us last season. Even if there were holes in our game, because everyone was working hard it gelled together so that it looked as though we were impenetrable. If someone had a weakness, someone else would be covering it. That's a sign of a good team. If I miss a tackle, I know my opponent's not going to get far, because there is always someone else coming across.

We were pretty rock solid again versus Italy. We managed another clean sheet in terms of tries. And although we had to work hard for our own tries, they came in the end. Jamie's touchdown gave us breathing space and then Alex Cuthbert sprinted home to seal the win late on.

Alex came from pretty much nowhere to be one of the stars of the Six Nations, scoring three tries in all. I remember the first time I saw him was about two years earlier, when I was out having a meal and one of the boys said hello to him. He knew him because he was on the Sevens circuit. I didn't know a lot about him. I just remember thinking what a big guy he was, especially for a wing. He only started playing for the Blues last season, but he soon caught the eye with his try-scoring and forced his way into the Wales squad. He loved being in that environment, playing with that calibre of players, and he went from strength to strength.

I think he's only going to get better. I thought he was a lot older than me when I first saw him, but in fact he's more than two years younger! I just can't believe how quick he is. I would back him one on one against anyone. And powerful. When we work in the gym, the forwards are usually renowned for being a lot stronger, but some of the backs are lifting bigger weights than us. They are so young coming through, as well. It's very good for Welsh rugby.

With Alex scoring late on, we ended up winning 24–3 and we were happy with the result. It was 'job done' in terms of moving a step closer to the Grand Slam. But we knew the performance hadn't been up to scratch. There were a lot of errors in the game. It was something we had to put right because we knew we would need a far more clinical performance against France if we were to complete the Slam.

Chapter Six

SEALING THE SLAM

There had been a lot of hype surrounding us ever since coming back from the World Cup, but it reached a new level ahead of the France game. I'd never experienced anything like it. There was a lot more media interest, but we didn't want to treat the run-up any differently from earlier weeks. The previous year, when we went out to France for the final game of the championship, the boys had said to the coaches that they felt a bit tired, and as a result we had a lighter week, and ended up getting slaughtered. So after the Italy game, Warren Gatland said that wasn't going to happen again and to be ready for a hard week. We had some tough training. We treated it no different to what we had done for any of the other games. We had to make sure we played well. But it was good preparation. I remember that the last team run was quite relaxed, but we were ready. We'd taken our defence coach Shaun Edwards's advice to keep cool heads, and not get wound up too early. It's all about switching on at the right time.

The match day was brilliant, especially driving into Cardiff on the team coach. Westgate Street was packed. We had the horses walking in front of the bus. It's mad how you always pick out one or two people from the crowd that you know. It may be someone you played rugby with once, or a cousin, or a family friend. They just happen to be there. The drive-in means such a lot. It really sets the mood.

A lot of us had never beaten France before, so it seemed a massive challenge but one we were really looking forward to. We were going out there to get a win and hoping it would be a huge occasion for us. And I was really looking forward to the challenge of playing against the French back row.

I remember it was quite warm inside the Millennium Stadium. I started off wearing my scrum cap, but I soon had to chuck it because it was so hot I started to feel stifled. As it turned out, it was one of those games where everything just went right for me and I ended up getting Man of the Match. Everything seemed to fall into place. When I went to make a tackle, even if my timing was out a bit I still ended up clipping them and they would fall over. It was a really tight game, with just the one try, Alex

Cuthbert scoring another great touchdown in the first half, and putting us in front.

I was absolutely exhausted going in at half-time. I'd taken a couple of hits to the head and I couldn't really see properly. I'd split my nose and my eye. So I can't tell you what Warren and Shaun Edwards were saying at half-time because I was getting stitched up on the bed.

I remember they injected my nose to stitch it, but when it came to my eye they asked if they could just do it. I said go on then. So I was getting my eye stitched up on the bed without anaesthetic. I got off the bed and tried to go back to my place and was a bit light-headed. I was in a bit of a state, really, but knew I had to dig deep. That's what it's all about. My former captain at the Dragons, Luke Charteris, used to sum it up quite well in his team-talk. He said, 'It's eighty minutes of pain you've got to put yourself through.' I remember thinking: 'This is forty minutes of pain I've got to dig in for.' So that's what I did.

All the boys dug deep. We were just not going to let that lead slip and, minute by minute, the Slam got closer and closer. Finally the clock reached eighty minutes.

Rhys Priestland kicked the ball out, the

whistle went and I was on my knees. All the boys were jumping around and going mad. I remember our fitness trainer, Dan Baugh, came running on and gave me a hug. I must admit I did get pretty emotional for a moment.

To win a Grand Slam was an incredible feeling. It was the third one Wales had won in eight years, but before that they had gone twenty-seven years without winning one. I remember Scott Quinnell saying he was jealous because he never had a chance to win a Slam. For me to have done something that such a legend in a game hasn't done really puts it in perspective. It's something to really treasure.

Because I was Man of the Match, I was interviewed live on television straight after the game. When I was interviewed I was just looking all round, everywhere but at the interviewer. I was trying to take it all in. Trying to savour those moments. I was so chuffed. It was a great feeling.

A lot of my friends from back home had been watching the game in a bar in Cardiff city centre. I was on the big screen in the pub, being interviewed, and they were trying to ring my phone and text me, which is quite funny, looking back. I've looked at a few of the pictures of me walking round the stadium after the game and I'm just staring up at the stands and around. You try to take it in as best you can. It was an awesome experience and I was just drained by the end of it. But the blood sweat and tears we'd put into it almost made it that much more special.

We went up to get the trophy, and standing there was a big moment. It meant all the more to me that my family was there, and to see them after the game was brilliant. We went to the Hilton Hotel for the after-match dinner and a big crowd of fans had gathered there. As we walked through everyone was tapping us and saying well done. Because we won, the after-match speeches went on for ages. I remember nearly falling asleep because I was so shattered from the game.

The boys were going for a few drinks after the match to celebrate but I didn't feel like drinking because I was so shattered and beat up from the game. I just wanted to go to bed.

I did stay out until about 1 or 2 o'clock, but then went back to the Vale. I was just so tired.

The next day I felt as if I'd been run over by a bus. But it was worth it. The scars and bruises all heal, and they can never take away the fact we won the Grand Slam. I am really proud to be part of that.

I do enjoy just playing rugby, but at the top level you also want to achieve things. That's what pushes you on and makes you a better player. And what better than to be able to say, 'I'm a Grand Slam winner!'

I know that when I hang up my boots and finish playing that I will get huge satisfaction from it. I will be able to look back and think, 'That was awesome.'

Chapter Seven

GRAND SLAM AFTERMATH

The day after we won the Grand Slam, I went into my local supermarket in Newport to pick up a few groceries and an old couple came up to me. They said well done for yesterday, and the old lady put her hand out to shake my hand. As I went to shake it, she turned mine over and kissed me on the hand. I was looking round and thinking, 'I hope no one saw that!' I didn't know how to react to it. I didn't know whether to do it back. So I just said thank you, and walked off.

That was the moment I realised things might be a bit different from now on. We knew there had been a real buzz back home during the World Cup, especially with the Millennium Stadium opening up for everyone to watch the semi-final against France. But we hadn't experienced it ourselves because we were over in New Zealand. This time it was different, because we were back home.

People really got behind Wales during the

Six Nations. I think there was a real feel-good factor within the country. People were going into work on that Monday morning after the Grand Slam with smiles on their faces and a spring in their step, just because we did it, and I think that's really great.

The Dragons gave me a week off playing, which was good because the championship had taken its toll on me. It had been so physical and I felt battered. So I was thankful for the break to let my body recover, but it was still a pretty hectic time off the field.

Because we had won the Slam, the whole of the Wales squad was invited to the Senedd – the National Assembly building – in Cardiff Bay for a civic reception. I had never been there before and didn't know what to expect. But it was brilliant. I think about 10,000 people turned up! It just shows how much people appreciated what we did. It was a great feeling.

You get to meet a lot of nice people in rugby, especially when you go out to different clubs and grounds. People are really friendly, and they all want to say well done.

A couple of days after the France game, Sara from the Dragons rang me up and said, 'Congratulations, you've won the RBS Player of the Tournament.' She said, 'I've got the award in a box here, so come down for a picture.' I agreed and asked who was giving it to me. She said, 'I will if you want.' I said, 'Brilliant!' So I received it from her.

I was really surprised to get the award and genuinely chuffed. It was a massive honour to win, especially given the quality of the other players up for the award. I was really grateful to everyone who voted for me. I don't usually pick up any Man of the Match awards, so to do it at international level and to get two of them in the Six Nations, and then the Player of the Tournament, meant a massive amount. It topped off an amazing competition for me.

It makes me think just how far I've come since I started out in international rugby. In my first start against Australia in 2010, I was really shocked by the speed of the game and I felt like I was chasing shadows. But then, the following year, I played against them again and knew what to expect. It was the same when I stepped up from semi-pro to regional level; the more you play the more you know what to expect, and you slowly get into it. Then you start building on your performances and that's what I've tried to do all my career. When I finish playing rugby I will look at the Six Nations award on the mantelpiece with pride but the thing I will take away and savour more than anything is being involved with that bunch of boys at that time. For so many of us young guys, it was our first time winning anything and we were all so delighted.

What we have achieved as a group of players is testament to the hard work that everyone puts in, not just the players, but the back room staff and everyone involved. The calibre of players means you pick things up from them, players like Ryan Jones, Gethin Jenkins or someone else. The whole Wales squad has real ambition and we all want to be the best we can be. There's a never-say-die attitude within the group and it's a fantastic environment. Of course, we know other nations are developing as well. I think that as long as we keep our heads down and work hard we will be fine, but it's important not to get carried away and we must never get ahead of ourselves. We really do have to take it game by game. That's certainly the way I approach it.

I do get asked quite often whether my life has changed since the Grand Slam and the Six Nations award and whether I get more attention now. The answer is that things have changed a bit, but it hasn't been a problem. When we came back from the World Cup in 2011, Sam Warburton got a lot of recognition in terms of people coming up to him when he was out, but nobody seemed to bat an eyelid at me! Now, I do get people stopping me in the street – and in the supermarket! In the last couple of games of the Six Nations, I'd taken my scrum-cap off because I'd been too hot, so maybe that's why people started recognising me!

So, yes, I do get recognised more now since the Grand Slam, but I don't mind it. Everyone who comes up and wants a chat is really friendly. And we all appreciate people saying well done, and telling us we're really good at what we do. We all like a pat on the back and a bit of praise.

I remember last summer I went home to mid-Wales when the local carnival was on. I was catching up with a few old school mates there, but every couple of minutes I was tapped on the back and asked to pose for a picture. My mates said, 'Doesn't that annoy you?' And it is sometimes hard when you are trying to have a conversation, but as long as everyone is friendly I really don't mind, especially with younger kids. It wasn't so long ago I was there wanting autographs myself. I remember going to the Royal Welsh Show near Builth Wells when the Scarlets were there one year and getting my picture taken with Scott Quinnell and Stephen Jones. (It's weird to think I've now played alongside Stephen for Wales. Weird, but brilliant.)

So while I certainly don't go looking for the limelight, it does mean a lot to have the backing and support of the public, and it was great to see how much the Grand Slam meant to people in Wales.

Chapter Eight

DISAPPOINTMENT DOWN UNDER

Having been crowned champions of Europe, the next challenge for us was to win in the southern hemisphere. We had the opportunity when we headed Down Under to take on Australia in a three Test series last summer. We went out there full of confidence. Even though it had been a long season, we were looking forward to getting back together as a squad. We always knew it was going to be tough down there and not many teams go to the southern hemisphere and get results. But we were definitely up for it and really excited about getting stuck into them.

Playing the Aussies on their own turf would see us move right out of our comfort zone. We were used to playing them at the Millennium Stadium where everyone was always behind us. But playing down there was just what we needed in terms of taking up the next challenge and pushing us on.

It would be huge for us if we could get a scalp. And playing the best in the world was the only way we were going to find out how good we were.

It had obviously been a long season, what with the build-up to the World Cup. But none of the players would ever turn down the opportunity to wear the red jersey. Every time you play, you know it could be your last time and that makes you want to give everything.

The opening Test was in Brisbane and I found that game really hard, especially the first half.

I hadn't played for six weeks and for some of the boys it was longer. In that first half we were all really blowing – it was so difficult getting up to speed again. That was one of the first times we almost felt we'd been outplayed. I didn't like that. But the Wallabies were already into their Super 15 rugby season, so they'd hit the ground running.

The Aussie skipper David Pocock is always going to win turnovers, but in that first game he was making loads of them. I remember going in for half-time and Shaun Edwards telling us that we'd all been there before. He said that we'd got the shock out of our system now. So we came out for the second half and seemed to get into the game more. Even when we were behind we had the same positive feeling as in the Six Nations, thinking we were going to win, but it wasn't to be this time.

However, we had a chance to make amends a week later in Melbourne. You always go out to prove yourself, but in that second Test we had even more to prove.

We got off to a really good start. George North scored a try pretty much straight away and we were off and running. It was a close game all the way through, but with just a couple of minutes to go we were still in front.

What happened next was hard to take. They were awarded a penalty, kicked to touch, set up the lineout drive and we were penalised for bringing it down. Then we just had to wait as their replacement Mike Harris lined up the penalty to win the game. It was out of our hands. They had missed one just before, so there was hope. But, fair play to him, he slotted it. We saw the kick sail over and our hearts sank. In the Six Nations at the end of the Ireland game, Leigh Halfpenny had slotted a penalty to win the game for us and now it was our turn to be on the receiving end.

It was hard to swallow, thinking we had almost done it, only to lose the match right at the death. There were eighty minutes up on the clock, and the hooter had sounded. We had put so much into the game. Blood sweat and tears had gone into it. We were shattered, devastated. It was tough in the changing room afterwards.

Rob Howley, who was standing in as caretaker coach for the injured Warren Gatland, said he couldn't have asked for anything more from us in terms of effort. And, yes, we had given it our all. We'd battled hard and it was a definite improvement on the previous week. But we had lost the series and we were gutted. We are a close bunch and it really did hurt. We are as big Welsh supporters as anyone back home and to come so close and still not get it was hard to take.

It is an honest environment within the camp and we had meetings after the game and reviewed the tape of the game, as we always do. The video is up on the screen and you are asked what you were thinking at the time and what would you do again in the same situation. It's hard to watch when it's you on screen, if you've missed a tackle for them to score, or given away a crucial penalty. You don't want to be the one up there.

But everyone makes mistakes. No one has a perfect game. A lot of it is down to the opposition you are playing against. They are trying to spoil your attack and you are trying to do exactly the same to them. It's the way it is. The main thing is that you learn from it.

After that Melbourne game the coaches gave us three days off to clear our heads, and then we went into the last Test in Sydney. We still had something to prove. Although we'd lost the series, we still wanted to get a scalp out there. To salvage something from the trip.

We had chances again, but made just too many errors. Credit to the Aussies, they took their chances well and kicked their points. It was our last opportunity and it wasn't good enough.

I was again absolutely gutted. We'd been getting closer and closer. We'd lost by eight points, then two, then one. But we still lost. When you play these big teams, you've got to perform the best you can and take your chances. We'd had chances to win all three games, but hadn't taken them and that was hugely disappointing.

Australia are a quality side and to come so close to beating them showed we had been making progress and weren't a million miles off it. But we want to be winning games out there.

In international rugby, it's those three points that make the difference. One penalty less in each of the games, and it might have been a different story.

I was so disappointed we couldn't get a result out there, but it was still a good experience because I'd never played in Australia before. To go up against their back row, which was really formidable, was a fantastic challenge. I learned a lot and I found myself coming back home with a lot more confidence, despite the results.

I was also relieved I didn't have to have an ankle operation when I got home. I'd been troubled by it for a while, but I went away to Australia and the injury somehow healed itself. One day I woke up and I didn't have any pain in it any more, which was brilliant.

I came back home, saw the surgeon and he said if it didn't hurt there was no point in having an operation. So that at least was one result that went my way Down Under.

But, as fate would have it, it wasn't too long before I did find myself going in for surgery – on the other ankle. Only a few weeks into the new season I broke my left leg just above the ankle while playing for the Dragons against

Edinburgh. So, once again in my career, I found myself facing a lengthy lay-off and a fight to get back to fitness.

Chapter Nine

CASE FOR THE DEFENCE

I guess I've become renowned for my tackling more than any other aspect of my game.

But when I was younger I liked to get the ball in my hands and carry it. That's what I loved doing.

However, I think that's something I've gone away from now. I've developed into being more of a defensive player.

I would like to add more ball-carrying into my game as time goes on. It's something I want to work on. But when you are being picked largely for your tackling ability, you've got to be careful not to undermine that. I don't want to take away from my strengths. I don't want to start making fewer tackles to try and free myself up to carry. So although I would like to be out there carrying, I'm also very aware what my main job for the team is. I go out there to try to make as many tackles as I can and be as destructive as possible, because that's me being most effective for the team. I always want to be right up there in the tackle count, and I'm disappointed if I am not. It's one of my goals and how I judge if I have had a decent game. Tackling is what I do, so if my tackle count is high, I know I've done my job. And if I can get a couple of good tackles in where the ball is spilt, or where I slow the opposition down so my team-mates can get in and win the ball, I think that's almost as good as someone making a 20-yard break.

I guess it's this ability at defence that people have focused on ever since I started to play regularly for the Dragons. Quite early on, our coach at the time, Paul Turner, dubbed me the White Samoan. I'm assuming that's because he felt I tackled like a Samoan. They tend to give it everything when they hit someone! You do get some random nicknames chucked at you and none of them really stick, but perhaps that one was prophetic.

It was when I came into the Welsh squad that my defensive game developed further, and a lot of that was down to our defence coach, Shaun Edwards.

When I first met him, I didn't quite know how to take him. I obviously knew he was a legend in rugby league but at first he came across as a really hard-nosed kind of guy. I think we have built a good working relationship. Shaun is fantastic. I have learnt a lot from him and I hope I can continue to do so and keep improving.

He's said some nice things about me and I value compliments from him because I have a lot of respect for him and what he does for the team. Most importantly, what he has done with Wales is to make sure that when we take the field everyone knows his role.

In every lineout, in every scrum, everyone knows where he should be. The right people are always in the right positions. We have drilled it so much that it's like second nature now.

We worked particularly hard on defence when we were gearing up towards the World Cup in 2011 and that's when we developed what has now become known as the chop tackle. Our first game in the tournament was going to be against South Africa and they are renowned for being big, powerful men who love to bash their way through the opposition. So Shaun put in a policy of trying to stop them before they got going. That meant hitting them fast, hitting them hard and hitting them low. The idea was that this would then enable the likes of Sam Warburton to get in on the tackled player and win the ball off him.

Well, we played that first game against the Springboks in Wellington and I can't remember how many turnovers Sam had. The boys were stopping the 'Boks in their tracks and that seemed to expose the ball for Sam to get on it. It worked so well that we thought, 'Hang on a minute, we might be on to something here.'

So we carried on with the policy and it was when we played against Ireland in the quarter-finals that it really came into its own. We knew how big and powerful their back row was and how good they were at carrying. We felt that if we could nullify their back row we would have a good chance of doing something. It worked really well and we won the match. That was probably the most enjoyable game I played in at the World Cup. When you've played well as a team, and as an individual, it's a really good feeling.

The chop-tackle tactic evolved from then. We carried it on into the Six Nations and I guess it's something I've become known for. On last summer's tour of Australia, I had a few collisions with the veteran Wallaby second row Nathan Sharpe. Every time I lined up in defence, he seemed to be coming around the corner with the ball, so he was always getting it. I kept on hitting him, chopping him down at the ankles. I remember we were at the bottom of a ruck one time and he said, 'Take it easy, I don't want my legs broken!' He came up to me at the end of the game as well and said, 'Take it easy on me next week.'

But then when we played the final Test in Sydney, they started chopping us as well! It's evolution. You learn things off the opposition, and they learn things off you.

The game is so physical now and there are such big men playing. Every back row you come up against these days usually has one massive ball-carrier. South Africa and Ireland both had three at the World Cup. If you can stop those players before they get on their bullocking runs it does help. So it's all about trying to get off the line as quick as you can and hitting them as low as you can.

Playing in the back row is always geared around being physical. You don't want someone to be carrying you up the field and making yards while you are trying to knock them down. If you are playing against a big ball-carrier, you don't want to give him a massive run-up because you don't want to be flat on your back as he is running past you. You have to make sure you chop him down before he gets going, so scavengers like Sam and Gethin can get in there, and that is what I try to do.

We always analyse teams and identify who their main threats are. If there is a certain strike runner or power player who can cause carnage, we will make sure we keep an eye on him.

I know I am not as skilful as some other players, but I also know I have a role to play in the team. In a way I'd rather be scoring the tries, but someone has to do what I do, so I am happy to do that. It's my job to stop the opposition and it is the job of George North, Alex Cuthbert and whoever else to score the tries. I'm not complaining. Everyone has a role to play in the team. Defence isn't as glamorous as scoring tries, and I don't know if people realise how much effort goes into it. Say you make twenty tackles in a game, that's twenty times you are torpedoing yourself at someone who is running really fast at you. Then you've got to pick yourself back up off the floor, get back in line and do it again.

In the past people asked me whether I ever worried about throwing myself into a tackle, given that I broke my neck while playing when I was younger. I'm told I looked a bit edgy on the field when I first came back from that injury. But I've talked to the same people since and they say now that they can see I am flying into tackles and that I don't care.

The way I look at it, I am a physical player and if I am not going to be physical, I might as well not be on the field. You don't always get it right and you feel knocked out if it goes wrong. But when it goes right, you think, 'I wonder what that looked like back on telly, because it felt good!'

For me, there's no better feeling than getting a tackle spot on. Making a big hit is what gives me my satisfaction in the game.

Chapter Ten

LIFE ON THE FARM

I was born in Salford, near Manchester, in December 1987. We lived there for a few years until I was about three or four and then we moved to mid-Wales, where my mother had grown up. My parents wanted to move out of the rat race. Where we moved to wasn't far from where my grandparents lived and they were farming at the time.

My brother Jack and I were really keen to help on the farm and we spent lots of time there. Then when my granddad reached retirement age, he told my parents he wanted me and my brother to have the farm when we were older. But for that to happen, my parents would have to run it in for the meantime, until we were at an age where we could take over. So my parents agreed and we moved to the farm when I was about six or seven. My mum, Lynne, has always been a farmer. It was her side of the family that owned the farm and my brother and I are fifth generation farmers in the family. My dad had been a dock worker. He'd worked at moving the big containers in the container base in Manchester. But together they took the farm over and it was a good place to grow up.

When I was starting out with the Dragons and travelling down to Newport to play games, I would always look forward to the trip home because I knew I was going back to the farm. However, after a while, I moved down to live in Cardiff and I found that hard to start with. Just seeing street-lights and hearing the sound of people and vehicles outside the house at midnight was hard to get used to.

If there was a vehicle about at midnight back at the farm, they would be stealing your farm quad or something! It's just peace and quiet there. So I did find it hard to adjust. To start with, I would come down on Sunday night, train in the week, drive back on Friday night and have the weekend on the farm. But the more I progressed in rugby the less I was able to go home. However, when I do get the chance to go back, I take it. If we have a Friday night game at Rodney Parade, I jump straight in the car and go back. It's just a chance to get away. It's what I enjoy. It's completely different from the day job. It's my peace and quiet, my release.

The farm is in a little place called Abbey-cwm-hir, near Llandrindod Wells. It's an average-size farm on a hillside, about 500 acres, and there's a lot to get through. It's a sheep farm. We've got about 700 sheep. My granddad had cattle, but we've just got sheep, although my brother would like to keep a few cows in the future, like my granddad did. Jack, who is two years older than me, basically runs the farm, but he and my mother and father all work together and I join in whenever I'm home.

Life on the farm depends on the season. Lambing is all sort of hours and during Six Nations time, they tend to be busy lambing, so everyone has to help. At that time of year, they work in shifts. My brother gets up at 5am and they don't finish until 11pm. But they still take time out to watch me play on television. Then when I get back home, I get stuck in too.

There will be days when it's really hard work, but then we all come in and Mum lays on a massive feast and we sit round the table, have good food and go to bed happy. We're quite close as a family. I ring my dad, John, every day for a chat. He is Salford born and bred and a Manchester United fan. Football is very much the sport on his side of the family. My cousin,

Jason Lydiate, played for Manchester United reserves in the same team as Ryan Giggs and went on to play for Blackpool, as well as other clubs.

But I was never going to be a footballer. You'd know why if you saw me kick a ball! My dad only got into rugby because my brother and I started playing, but he's a fan now. Being English-born, he obviously wants England to do well. When we play England, he sings both the anthems. But he supports me at the end of the day and I think he would rather see Wales win the Six Nations than England.

My parents have been great, right behind me since I started playing. They have also brought me up to be the person I am. They have taught me to value things, such as that good manners cost nothing, but they mean the world. It's a big thing in our family, always being polite to people, treating them as you would like to be treated yourself.

I think my upbringing has also helped me with my rugby. There's a lot of manual labour on the farm. It's more mechanical now, but when my parents took over it was all about lugging hay bales around and things like that. In the winter, you are always loading up quad bikes with these bales and feeding the sheep. You also spend a lot of time trying to catch sheep and they will fight with you as hard as they can. All farmers can tackle because they are used to chasing sheep. Unless you've got a good dog, you are on your own chasing them down. That's probably where my tackling ability comes from!

Being back on the farm is a real refuge for me. That's why I enjoy going back so much. Players do have off games and you do beat yourself up about them, but going back there you can put it out of your mind. I'll say to my parents that I don't want to talk about it, and we'll just have a cup of tea and talk about everyday life instead.

So, when I get a couple of days off I go back there and find it's a great place to clear my head. I can get back in touch with reality and I always feel better for going there. I really enjoy that part of my life and I think it's something I'll always go back to. I would like to have a long career in rugby, but you never know these days. I'll try to make the most of it for the time being, but I will always want to move back to the farm because I really enjoyed my upbringing there. It will be nice to maybe have a family of my own there. Playing rugby is not a job for life. I'm just a farming lad from mid-Wales and that's what I'll be doing full-time when the rugby ends.

Chapter Eleven

DREAMING OF LIONS

One of my first rugby memories is of watching the British & Irish Lions tour of Australia in 2001. I wasn't playing much rugby at the time. I was thirteen and only just getting into it. But when something like that is on the telly, of course you watch it.

I remember Scott Quinnell scoring a try in the first Test in Brisbane and him just nodding and smiling after he touched down. But what I really remember is the England flanker Richard Hill playing for that Lions team and thinking to myself, 'He's somewhere I want to be.' He was my rugby hero growing up. I liked the fact that he was just a real dog. You would see him being interviewed after a game and his face would be beat up to hell but he'd be doing exactly the same the next week.

He was hugely respected by his fellow players. I remember an interview one of the England backs gave once and he was asked who would be the first name on his team-sheet. He said Richard Hill. The average man on the street, who just watches rugby when the Six Nations is on, knows Shane Williams and those sorts of people. But the die-hard rugby fan would notice the work that this guy Hill was doing. He was a vital cog in the England team that won the World Cup in 2003 and for me, growing up, he was the player I really looked up to and tried to model myself on. So when Shaun Edwards likened me to him last year, it was amazing. I couldn't ask for a bigger compliment.

To my mind, the turning point of that 2001 Lions tour was when Hill was injured midway through the second Test. Up to that point, the Lions had been on top in the series, but without Hill they went on to lose 2–1. I guess I studied him all the more because I was playing in the same position as him. I was playing flanker for Builth Wells U14s at the time.

The main reason I had started out playing was because my brother Jack was playing rugby for Builth and he played back row. You always look up to your older brothers and sisters. And Richard Hill was his favourite player as well. So you take it all on board and when I saw Hill playing for the Lions in 2001, I knew that's what I wanted to do.

Now things have come full circle and the Lions are going to be touring Australia again this year. Obviously I'd love to be part of that trip. The Lions is the ultimate for a British rugby player. The pinnacle.

A couple of years ago, the pinnacle for me was playing for Wales. I've been given the chance to do that and it's meant the world to me. But once you do that, your goals move on, and to play for the Lions is now a major goal.

It's a really big year with that tour of Australia coming up at the end of the season.

But I never try to look too far ahead and given what happened to me at the start of this season, there's no way I can. Playing against Edinburgh in September, I went to make a tackle and fell back awkwardly, breaking my left leg just above the ankle. Initially, I feared that I'd suffered a fracture and dislocation which would have meant me being out for the whole season. It wasn't quite that bad, but I still needed surgery and I was faced with being out of action for four to five months. That meant I was out of the autumn internationals and was facing a race against time to get back for any of this year's Six Nations. So the challenge of making the Lions tour is now even greater.

Having toured Australia with Wales last summer, it would be great to go back out there.

I didn't get to see that much of the country, other than from the air, because there was a lot of travelling and we had a busy schedule. But in the last week we did have a bit of time off, and it was great to go round Sydney and see the sights. The whole trip was a wonderful experience on and off the field.

I think it was good for us going to Australia, because the Welsh boys that do go on the Lions tour will know what to expect from the country. And they will also be all the keener to go, with Warren Gatland having been appointed Lions coach.

Warren has been brilliant for us. He has brought a lot of younger boys through and we are allowed to play what is in front of us. Obviously, we have our set moves, but he always tells us, 'Back yourself, you are good enough players, so go out and play.' It's a good feeling to go out there with the freedom to have a go and know that, whether it's the right decision or the wrong decision, as long as you give it your best shot, the coaches will support you. So to play under 'Gats' for the Lions would be a great experience.

Therefore, it's all the more frustrating to have picked up a pretty serious injury at the start of this season. However, the injury aside, I couldn't be any happier with my lot. I'm treated really well at the Dragons. I can't thank them enough for what they've done for me, especially in the early days of my career. They gave me the chance to play top-flight rugby and put myself on show to the Welsh selectors. Maybe if I had been at another club I might not be playing international rugby. They are understanding about bumps and bruises, so if you have to miss a session they don't mind, as long as you put it in once you are on the field.

I've loved it with the Dragons and I love playing for Wales. I wouldn't say I'm a perfectionist, but rugby is a short career. No one is going to play for ever, so you've got to try and make the most of it while you are here. Personally, I just want to get as many caps as I can. I want to play as much as I can for Wales because I'm enjoying it so much.

I hope I'm still developing as a rugby player and I'll keep working on certain aspects of my game to become better. It's vital to do so because if you stand still you are going to get overtaken.

I also know, from personal experience, that

you have to savour every minute. My brother Jack, who went on to play for Ebbw Vale, had to quit rugby after badly breaking his leg. And, of course, my career could have ended before it really began with the neck injury I suffered out in France.

And, as I write this book, I am once again recovering from injury after breaking my leg. So, for me, it's a case of making the most of every moment and recognising just how very lucky I am.

Quick Reads 📖

Books in the Quick Reads series

Quick Reads

Fall in love with reading

Peak Performance
Tori James

Accent Press

Everest: the highest mountain in the world and also one of the most dangerous.

On May 24 2007, Tori James made history when she became the first Welsh woman, and youngest British woman, to climb to the summit of Everest. It was an amazing achievement for the petite farmer's daughter from Pembrokeshire. In *Peak Performance* Tori shares the inspiration and drive that helped her to succeed in reaching the 'rooftop of the world'.

Quick Reads 📖

Fall in love with reading

Finding Myself Lost
Richard J Oliver

Accent Press

In the summer of 2000 Richard Oliver, better known as Jamie, was making a name for himself as an artist. One day he announced, 'I've decided to join a band'. Following every young man's dream, he bought himself a set of turntables and a week later played his first show with Lostprophets. Told they would never sell more than 4,000 records, the band released their first album to great success. More than a decade later, Lostprophets continue to be one of the UK's most successful rock bands. With five best-selling albums and numerous awards to their name, they sell out tours all over the world.

In *Finding Myself Lost* Richard reveals what really goes on behind the scenes on the road and reflects on his own personal growth along the way.

Quick Reads 📖

Fall in love with reading

Hostage
Emlyn Rees

Accent Press

Hostage retrieval expert. Danny Shanklin, the hero of *Hunted*, returns in this spin-off short-paced thriller.

Mary Watts, the wife of rich mogul, Richard Watts, has been kidnapped.

Haunted by the death of his wife and daughter, murdered in front of his eyes by the notorious Paper Stone Scissors killer, Danny is hired to find her before the kidnapper's carry out their threat of execution.

But the raid goes wrong and Danny is left for dead.

Can he find Mary before her kidnappers? And will he be able to save her?

Quick Reads

Fall in love with reading

Earnie: My Life with Cardiff City
Robert Earnshaw

Accent Press

From the African plains to the Millennium Stadium, this is the remarkable story of the boy who was born to be a Bluebird.

Nicknamed Earnie, this is the story of Robert Earnshaw's journey from the Zambian village where he was born to Caerphilly, where he first kicked a 'proper' football. Seven years later, aged 16, he was signed up by Cardiff City and started banging in the goals on his way to break the Bluebirds' goal-scoring records.

Here Earnie reflects on his Welsh success, his trademark somersault goal celebration and the crazy world of Sam Hammam, and he reveals why Cardiff City will always have a special place in his heart.

Quick Reads 📖

Fall in love with reading

Going for Gold

Accent Press

What does it take to go for gold and be the greatest?

In *Going For Gold*, Wales's leading athletes share the secrets of their drive and determination to be the best in their sport.

Cyclist Geraint Thomas, who won Olympic gold in the Team Pursuit in Beijing 2008, and 11 times gold medal-winning paralympic swimmer Dave Roberts talk of their ambitions to win in London 2012.

World champion hurdler David 'Dai' Greene explains his hunger to be the best and the importance of loving what you do, while Commonwealth medal-winning swimmer Jazmin 'Jazz' Carlin and paralympic world champion Nathan Stephens reveal the discipline needed to go for gold.

This collection of stories will inspire others to aim for their goals and follow their dreams.

Quick Reads 📖

Fall in love with reading

Why do Golf Balls have Dimples?
Wendy Sadler

Accent Press

Have you ever wondered why golf balls have dimples or why your hair goes frizzy in the rain?

Scientist Wendy Sadler has the answers in her book of Weird and Wonderful facts.

Broken down into user-friendly chapters like sport, going out, the great outdoors, food and drink and the downright weird, Wendy's book gives the scientific answers to life's intriguing questions, like why toast always lands butter-side down and why you can't get (too) lost with a satnav.

About the Author

Photo Huw Evans Agency

Welsh flanker Dan Lydiate grew up on his family's farm near Llandrindod Wells. He started his rugby career as a teenager with Newport Gwent Dragons Academy, progressing to their senior squad. In 2008 he suffered a serious neck injury in the Dragons' Heineken Cup Group match at Perpignan threatening his playing career. A year later he made his debut for Wales and quickly established himself as a key player.